Pio, Lugari, and Cuny

MIRACLES OF SPIRIT, COMMUNITY, AND CRISIS

JIM LOWENSTERN

Pio, Lugari, and Cuny

MIRACLES OF SPIRIT, COMMUNITY, AND CRISIS

JIM LOWENSTERN

Kravitz & Sons
INNOVATORS IN PUBLISHING, MARKETING AND ADVERTISING

Kravitz and Sons LLC
204 E Arlington Blvd. Suite B
Greenville, NC 27858

Published by Kravitz and Sons LLC.

| ISBN: | 979-8-89639-528-7 (sc) |
| ISBN: | 979-8-89639-529-4 (e) |

Library of Congress Control Number: 2025920544

INTRODUCTION

Ordinary Men, Extraordinary Impact

The Lives of Padre Pio, Paolo Lugari, and Fred Cuny

In a world too often shaped by conflict, inequality, and environmental destruction, it's easy to believe that only the powerful can make lasting change. But history tells another story: one shaped by the quiet resolve of individuals who, though seemingly ordinary, dared to confront extraordinary challenges. Among them stand Padre Pio, Paolo Lugari, and Fred Cuny; three men from different countries, different callings, and different eras, united by one unshakable conviction: that compassion, courage, and innovation can transform even the darkest of situations.

Padre Pio, a humble Capuchin friar in southern Italy, never left his monastery, yet reached the hearts of millions through his spiritual healing, deep empathy, and unwavering faith. Paolo Lugari, an unassuming Colombian visionary, took on the impossible by building a thriving, sustainable community, Gaviotas, in a barren savanna dismissed by experts as uninhabitable. Fred Cuny, an American engineer, chose not the safety of a desk but the frontlines of disaster, bringing clean water, shelter, and dignity to people trapped in war zones and refugee crises around the world.

None of them sought fame; none of them followed a script. But through their actions, rooted in faith, ethics, and bold reimagination of what was possible, they redefined what it means to serve humanity.

Exploring their lives helped me see just how powerful the actions of a single person can be. I was amazed by their courage, their innovation, and their deep commitment to others. And perhaps, as you learn about them too, you'll feel what I did: you don't just admire them; you're inspired to follow in their footsteps, in whatever way you can. Because the world still needs people like them. And maybe, just maybe, that person is you.

PADRE PIO

The Life of Padre Pio

Padre Pio was born May 25, 1887, and died September 23, 1968, at 81 years old.

Padre Pio became a Saint on June 16, 2002.

He had stigmata, a bleeding of palms (perhaps in sympathy with Jesus on the Cross). He was known to bilocate, and known (or in theory, he would fly near Allied planes during WWII, causing airplanes not to bomb near San Giovanni, where he was a friar. The bombs came back to base, causing problems with superior officers, and/or the bombs were released in vacant fields).

Consciousness Frontier was a metaphysical lecture series at the Vienna Baptist Church. I used to go to the day session on Wednesdays, also a night version on Tuesday night. I found a Jean Eek reference for an event at NOVA (Jr. College at Loudoun Campus), but the modern internet couldn't find the history of the excellent lecture series I attended.

I learned about Padre Pio from two presenters at this lecture series. I was raised Jewish (Dad's side left Germany in the nick of time) and Mother's side was Protestant, so I did not hear about Padre Pio from the Catholic legends, but by the Psychic presenters. Padre Pio was known to bilocate, and during World War II, he is believed to fly in the sky and startle pilots on bombing missions, and they didn't release their planes' bombs, and got in trouble for that, or bombed empty fields. The theory, or legend, or reality is Padre Pio was protecting where he lived, San Giovanni Rotondo.

There are several suspected incidents of bilocation with Padre Pio. One was in 1957, a month or two after I was born.

Padre Placido, who had an earlier interest in Padre Pio and had taken photos of Pio's hands and the stigmata on both palms, was in a hospital in San Severo and was worried he was going to die. Pio came to visit him and assured him he was going to recover. He lived 11 more years. Pio put his hand on a glass pane (in the hospital) that stayed hours later.

A Padre Alberto was visiting Padre Placido, and Placido proceeded to tell him (Alberto) about the Pio visit. Alberto doubted the truth of the visit, and Padre Placido begged Padre Alberto to go see Pio at San Giovanni. He did, and he asked Pio about the visit. Pio said it was true but not to tell anyone. Alberto told a lot of people about what may have happened.

(From Padre Pio: The True Story)

***

C. Bernard Ruffin

C. Bernard Ruffin (November 22, 1947 – May 4, 2019) was an American non-fiction author, as well as an educator, theologian, and pastor.

Partial list of books:

1. The Life of Brother Andre: The Miracle Worker of St. Joseph
2. The Days of the Martyrs: A History of the Persecution of Christians from Apostolic Times to the Time of Constantine
3. Padre Pio: The True Story

***

My Story About C. Bernard Ruffin

I first heard about Padre Pio in a lecture series by a woman named Jean Eek, at Vienna Baptist Church, which I lived across the street from. It was spiritual and metaphysical in nature (light years away from Baptist theology). Two different speakers mentioned Pio and his miracles. (After she died, Jean Eek, that was the end of the lecture series at the Baptist Church.)

I met C. Bernard Ruffin years later. We were taking a class at a NOVA campus (Jr. College, many campuses in Northern Virginia; I think it was the Alexandria Campus). I found out he had written a book on Padre Pio. I bought the book, and he autographed it:

To my friend Jim Lowenstern, with best wishes and God's blessings,

-Bernard Ruffin

My Favorite Padre Pio Story

Padre Pio had many people come to see him at San Giovanni. He had a fan club of women who were competitive with other visitors or worshippers. Maybe they wanted Padre Pio for themselves, and they could be rude to other pilgrims who visited and wanted attention or got in line for confession.

One day a brother and sister, perhaps young teenagers, took a train to see Padre Pio. Their parents tried to discourage them. Padre Pio would bleed from his palms—the sign of the Cross, feeling Jesus's torture on the Cross. The parents didn't believe or want their children to touch the blood or scars on Padre Pio's palms. They thought it was gross.

The two were among the crowd to see Padre Pio and saw others touch Padre's stigmata. When the two approached Padre Pio to touch, as others had, he looked at them and angrily scolded them: "Remember the promise you made to your parents not to touch." The two, brother and sister, startled and embarrassed, did not touch the palms as others in line did before. The two wondered, how did Padre Pio know?

General Bernardo Rosini of the United Air Command recounted that every time the pilots returned from their missions, they spoke of this friar appearing in the sky and turning their planes away.

General Nathan F. Twining of the USAF, who was in Bari, decided to personally lead a bombing mission near San Giovanni Rotondo. As they neared the target, both he and his squadron saw a monk with raised hands in the sky. Miraculously, their bombs dropped harmlessly into open fields.

Upon their return, there was widespread curiosity about the identity of the friar. The General and his pilots were informed about Padre Pio and decided to visit him. The pilots immediately recognized Padre Pio as the monk they had seen. Padre Pio addressed General Twining, saying, "So you are the one that wants to destroy everything." This encounter led to a friendship between the General (Twining) and Padre Pio.

Padre Pio, by one source, said planes malfunctioned, and bombs dropped in fields instead of buildings near San Giovanni Rotondo, where the friar Pio lived. Several pilots and crew claimed to see the flying monk, i.e., Pio.

***

Guided by Padre Pio: The Miraculous Presence, Bilocation, and Spiritual Journey of Giovanna

Padre Pio was known to have a beautiful scent that preceded him and was with him. The scent has been described as rose-like and by others tobacco-like, besides the bleeding of the palms, or stigmata, representing the pain Jesus felt on the Cross. There are various reports of Padre Pio bilocating. People try to do astral traveling a few steps or many before bilocation.

According to legend, one of the first bilocation events was January 18, 1905. Giovanni Battista Rizzani was dying. He was a non-believer, but his wife was, and she prayed a priest would administer last rites. Leonide (the wife's name) saw a vision of a young priest talking to her dying husband, and as he passed, she had a baby. A person who worked on the estate helped deliver the baby.

The family moved to Rome after her husband died. In 1922, in St. Peter's Basilica, the young girl born years earlier, Giovanna, was having a life crisis and wanted to go to confession. Padre Pio stated later he heard her confession and explained the Holy Trinity. A guard at the Basilica explained that the church was closed and the next day she could go to confession. She expressed to the guard that she had just confessed and wanted to thank the priest, and when the guard pulled the curtain, Pio was not there (or anyone else).

A year later, she, Giovanna, and a girlfriend went to San Giovanni. Padre Pio thanked her for coming to see him. She was surprised and had no idea who Pio was, and he explained he had been there when her father died and when she was born, and how he was there when she confessed in Rome a year before. For many years Padre Pio would end up giving Giovanna guidance. He told her he felt he had a responsibility to help her, and a few days before Padre Pio died, he said in a dream to her that she should see him soon before it was too late. She did travel to San Giovanni Basilica. He died soon afterwards.

She had been traveling to see and getting guidance from Padre Pio for many years as they both were getting older.

Instead of calling her name Giovanna, in this book she is GR.

A Padre Pio Profile
John A. Schig, OFM Cap.

The story at the chapel in Rome is slightly different. In this version, she sees a custodian who tells her that no one is there to hear her confession. She then sees Padre Pio, who agrees to hear her confession. The same issue arises, and Pio explains the Trinity to her, which helps her greatly. Later, the custodian sees her again and tells her to leave because no one is available to hear her confession. She protests, insisting that she had just confessed to a priest. When the custodian opens the door to the confessional, Padre Pio is no longer there—he had left through bilocation. This event took place in 1922.

In 1923, she and a friend went to San Giovanni Basilica, where Padre Pio lived and worked. Padre Pio saw her, greeted her, and told her that they had met before. She denied this, but he reminded her of the confession she made to him in Rome a year earlier. He also mentioned the event of her birth: her father had died and communicated with Padre Pio before she was born. Pio explained that he had heard her confession that day in Rome and felt a responsibility to help her.

A few days before Padre Pio died, he appeared to her in a dream, urging her to see him soon before it was too late. She traveled to San Giovanni Basilica, but shortly afterward, he passed away. For many years, as both of them grew older, she had continued visiting Padre Pio and receiving his guidance.

Though the details are sometimes told slightly differently, the accounts consistently describe the same story: the infant born as her father passed away, the miraculous confession in Rome in 1922, and her later encounters with Padre Pio at his home, where she at first did not recognize that they had met before.

Padre Pio's Stigmata and the Struggles of Sainthood

Padre Pio was in great demand for confessions, sometimes hearing them for 14 to 19 hours in a single day.

Church authorities above Pio in the hierarchy would occasionally suspend him from various tasks, including hearing confessions.

This may have been due to his popularity or his spiritual gifts—such as bilocation, the stigmata, the fragrance that emanated from him, or simply his widespread following—which some believed disturbed the status quo.

In May and June of 1960, the Bishop of Foggia (who outranked Pio) stated that 50,000 letters arrived each month from Italy alone, with an additional 24,000 coming from other countries. Other friars were assigned the task of reading these letters and passing along to Padre Pio only those they deemed most worthy of his attention.

In October of 1918, Padre Pio wrote that he had mixed feelings about his stigmata. He accepted the suffering willingly, but he struggled with the attention it brought him.

At one point, a surgeon named Luigi Romanelli, himself a Catholic, was asked by higher-ranking members of the Catholic Church to examine Padre Pio.

He examined Padre Pio regarding the stigmata five times between May 1919 and July 1920. He stated that he enjoyed the fragrance that seemed to emanate from Padre Pio, describing it as "an inebriating perfume," something many others also reported. He observed that the wounds showed no signs of festering or healing and concluded that they were "a phenomenon which human science could not explain."

After this, others investigated Padre Pio's stigmata, some with curiosity and reverence, while others reacted with hostility or suspicion, disturbed by what they could not understand.

***

Miracles and Healings Attributed to Padre Pio

A few miracles were also attributed to Padre Pio. In one instance, a young child was brought to him by his family. The boy had suffered from an illness at the age of four that left him with back problems, causing him to appear crooked and unable to stand straight. After meeting Padre Pio, the boy left standing upright, free of stiffness or back issues.

That same year, in 1919, a 62-year-old man who had been in an accident and suffered two broken legs came to Padre Pio. His legs had healed poorly, and he relied on two canes to walk. After hearing his confession, Padre Pio admonished the man and instructed him to throw away the canes. The man obeyed, and to his amazement, he was able to walk successfully without them.

In another case, a man suffering from great pain due to a swollen knee was scheduled by his doctor to receive a series of injections. Before beginning the treatment, he went to confession with Padre Pio. During the confession, he shared his pain, then continued with the rest of his penance. As he was leaving San Giovanni, he realized his knee was no longer swollen and the pain was gone. Rushing back, he tried to thank Padre Pio for the healing, but Padre Pio humbly told him, "Do not thank me. You need to thank God."

Two women with similar stories experienced remarkable healings. One had cancer in her intestine, and the other had a growth in her stomach. Both women went to confession with Padre Pio and told him they were scheduled to see a doctor. He encouraged each of them to proceed with their medical appointments. In both cases, when the doctors examined them, the illnesses were gone—the growths could no longer be found.

There are many anecdotes of Padre Pio noticing someone in a crowd and immediately knowing the person's struggle. Countless testimonies also describe healings that followed such encounters.

***

Bilocation: Padre Pio's Mysterious Presence Beyond San Giovanni

There are also numerous accounts of Padre Pio's bilocation, even though many witnesses stated that he rarely left San Giovanni.

One notable incident occurred in 1957, just a month or two after I was born. Padre Placido, who had previously shown interest in Padre Pio and photographed his stigmata, was hospitalized in San Severo and feared he was going to die. Pio appeared to him, reassured him he would recover, and indeed, Placido lived for another eleven years. During this visit, Pio placed his hand on a hospital glass pane, leaving an imprint that reportedly remained for hours afterward.

Padre Alberto, who was visiting Placido at the hospital, heard him describe the encounter with Padre Pio. Skeptical, Alberto later traveled to San Giovanni to ask Pio about it directly. Pio confirmed the visit but asked Alberto not to tell anyone. Despite this, Padre Alberto shared the story widely.

Padre Pio's Humor and Personal Encounters

Another account comes from Monsignor Damiani, Vicar General of the Diocese of Salto, Uruguay, who met Padre Pio as early as 1929. During their meeting, he asked Pio for last rites. Pio refused, telling him he would die in Uruguay. In 1942, as Monsignor Damiani lay dying, Padre Pio reportedly appeared in Uruguay through bilocation to give him the last rites he had once requested.

Andre Mandato wanted to move to the U.S. for a better future. He filled out an application for a permanent resident card. That night, Padre Pio appeared to him in a dream and told him that his application had been denied. In the same dream, Pio instructed him to reapply with a different sponsor. As foretold, Mandato's first application was denied, but his second—submitted with a new sponsor—was approved.

A couple struggled for many years to have children. The wife prayed to Padre Pio for a healthy baby. Near the time of delivery, she had a dream in which she was in a hospital room, attended by a doctor, while a man dressed as a friar—Padre Pio—stood quietly in the corner. The baby was later born healthy. Overjoyed, the wife wanted to take her husband and child to San Giovanni to see Padre Pio in person, or at least to confirm if it was really him she had seen in the dream. The husband agreed, though he remained skeptical. When the family arrived, they waited in a hallway where Pio would soon pass by. As he approached the husband, Pio gently patted his shoulder and teased him: "So it was all just a dream, eh?"

(Padre Pio was known to have a sense of humor.)

Another story tells of a priest who asked his superiors for permission to travel to San Giovanni to confess to Padre Pio. They agreed.

On the bus ride there, the priest fell asleep and dreamed that "the spiritual life, at times, seems like trying to climb glass." When he finally entered the confessional and completed his confession, Padre Pio looked at him and said: "So, the spiritual life seems like climbing glass?" (It was said that Pio chuckled gently as he said this.)

Padre Pio and World War II: Protecting San Giovanni from Bombing

Men flying planes during the war were assigned to release bombs over southern Italy, near San Giovanni. Some of these men were Protestants, but after encountering Padre Pio in person, they later converted to Catholicism. Witnesses claimed that Padre Pio appeared in the sky, preventing the planes from dropping their bombs. The planes returned to base with their payloads still intact—causing the crews to face trouble with their superiors. In other instances, bombs were released but fell harmlessly into empty fields.

A few of the airmen visited Padre Pio during the war, while many more came after the war ended. Several of them recognized him as the same figure they had seen in the sky, stopping the bombing of his area.

https://www.miraclesofthesaints.com/2010/09/bilocation-of-st-padre-pio.html#:~:text=Biloca

While the gift of bilocation has been attributed to countless saints, some of the most frequent and well-documented accounts occurred relatively recently in the extraordinary life of St. Padre Pio of Pietrelcina (1887–1968).

The Miracle of Last Rites: Padre Pio's Visit in New York

Here is another event: A family that had moved from Pietrelcina, where Padre Pio was born, later settled in Flushing, New York. In 1960, Grandfather Jack Crafa had been in a coma for 8 or 9 days. His granddaughter Ellie, then 31 years old, lived nearby with her parents and was at her grandfather's bedside at his house one night when there was a knock at the door.

A monk, dressed in sandals on a snowy day, stood outside. Ellie wondered why someone from the local church had not come instead. The visiting monk explained that he was there to pray for her grandfather. He prayed and encouraged the family to pray aloud with him as well.

He gave the man in the coma the Last Rites.

Ellie's father, James, saw the monk leave the house. There was no car waiting outside, and he disappeared into the night. Lucy, Ellie's mother and James's wife, noticed her husband looked disturbed or shaken and asked what was wrong.

James replied, "Don't you know who that was? It was Padre Pio. He came to give the Last Rites to your father, and he looked exactly like I remember him when I used to deliver eggs to him in Pietrelcina."

I cannot tolerate criticism and speaking ill of our neighbor. It is true, sometimes I enjoy teasing them, but speaking ill of them makes me sick. We have so many defects in ourselves to criticize—why pick on our neighbor? And lacking in charity, we damage the roots of the tree of life, with the risk of killing it.

– St. Padre Pio

https://aleteia.org/2024/05/01/10-fascinating-facts-about-padre-pio

From the source above, it is said that Padre Pio spent up to 17 hours a day helping or counseling people.

The same source also mentioned that Padre Pio prayed several hours each day.

https://padrepiodevotions.org/issue-54/

***

Padre Pio's Guidance: Love, Healing, and Faith

From another account:

A man once went to see Padre Pio. He told Padre Pio that his wife had just died and that he did not want to marry again. Padre Pio advised him that he should marry again and told him that when he returned, it would be as part of a couple.

Six years later, the man met a woman who had previously told Padre Pio in a dream that her mission was not to get married. Padre Pio then explained to her that marriage is also a mission. The man and the woman fell in love, got married, and later went together to see Padre Pio, just as he had foretold.

Giuseppe Di Sessa and Maria Grazia were the two people in the story above.

A woman named Maria Guerriero was working on a writing project that she intended to present to Pope Pius XII. The subject was the Assumption of the Blessed Virgin Mary. In August 1940, Maria's two sisters, Laura and Antonietta, went to see Padre Pio and told him about the project their sister Maria was undertaking. Padre Pio replied that if the Blessed Virgin had chosen Maria for this task, she must persevere with it, and he assured them that he would keep her in his prayers.

Maria dedicated herself deeply to this work but began to suffer from debilitating headaches. Her sisters wrote to Padre Pio about her condition. Soon after, Maria had a dream in which she went to see Padre Pio. A man opened the door to the building and explained that there was another area where confessions were held, but women were not allowed there. She asked again if he would request Padre Pio to see her, and he agreed.

The man later returned and led her into a room where Padre Pio came in, with blood dripping down the left side of his face. Maria thought to herself, *How selfish I am*. Padre Pio then tapped her on the head three times and told her she was cured.

She later wrote to Padre Pio, thanking him for her healing. He replied, giving credit to God and the Blessed Virgin Mary, and encouraged her to continue working on her project. On January 31, 1941, Maria placed her completed work on the desk of Pope Pius XII. That summer, Maria and her two sisters went to see Padre Pio. When he saw Maria, he tapped her on the head three times in the exact same place. She then asked him, "Am I still your spiritual daughter?" Padre Pio replied, "Yes, you are."

PAOLO LUGARI

THE LIFE OF PAOLO LUGARI

Paolo Lugari was born in Italy but has lived in Popayán, Colombia (his mother's homeland), since the age of four. A pioneer in biodiversity and the use of solar energy, he famously states,

"There is no energy crisis, only a crisis of imagination."

He is the founder of Las Gaviotas (Spanish for The Seagulls), a sustainable community established over 44 years ago on a vast plain, created in his search for energy solutions that would not harm the atmosphere. Lugari is an expert in sustainable development and renewable technologies and has been a speaker at numerous universities and academic institutions.

The United Nations University in Tokyo awarded him the Zero Emissions World Award. He also received Colombia's National Environment Award. His award-winning speeches, delivered on behalf of Colombia at the UN World Conference on Human Settlements and the Conference on Technical Cooperation Among Developing Countries, have had international impact. He was also a keynote speaker at a World Conference of the Club of Rome, a renowned global think tank.

LAS GAVIOTAS (The Seagulls)

Las Gaviotas is a non-profit foundation encompassing 11,000 hectares, 8,000 of which are covered with Caribbean tropical pine. Born in a region once considered barren, the community has become a world leader in sustainable development.

For Paolo Lugari, "Trees are the support of ecosystems."

Through reforestation and innovation, he has created stable, well-paid employment for a community of over 200 families, who live, eat, and are educated within Gaviotas.

His creative vision and tireless efforts have turned Las Gaviotas into a global model of sustainable development—one that continues to inspire communities and leaders around the world.

A Facebook post – Mentes Extraordinarias

https://www.google.com/search?q=inventions+made+at+Gavatios+used+in +other+parts+of+columbia&rlz=1C1GCEA_enUS977US977&oq=inventions+ made+at+Gavatios+used+in+other+parts+of+columbia&aqs=chrome..69i5 7j33i160l5.24765j0j7&sourceid=chrome&ie=UTF-8

Through effort and innovation, a solar water collector was developed. An estimated 31,000 units have been used throughout Colombia, including in Bogotá.

--

It is said that each house in Gaviotas has a device that generates electricity by running water through it. This is called a micro-hydro plant, and one estimate suggests that about 100 kilowatts are generated in total.

One of the windmills developed in Gaviotas is used as a pump to draw water from deeper underground. It utilizes a sleeve pump design. According to sources, this technology is now being used in other parts of Colombia as well.

Source: Google Search – Inventions made at Gaviotas used in other parts of Colombia

A variation of cement was also developed using the local soil from the region.

Source: Good Anthropocenes – Intentional Community in Gaviotas, Colombia

Through extensive tree planting, Gaviotas transformed the area from dry llanos (savannah) into a tropical forest.

Drinking water was also improved through better technology— including the use of filters and other systems.

Gaviotas maintained a strict no-firearms policy within their community—despite the challenges posed by surrounding rival factions, including left-wing anti-government guerrilla groups and militarized forces. When the hospital was still operating, people from surrounding areas were welcomed and received the medical care they needed.

Source:

Paolo Lugari's Vision: Creating Gaviotas in the Llanos

In 1971, Paolo Lugari gathered engineers and scientists to help form an intentional community named *Gaviotas*. It was located near a dry grassland area called the *Llanos*, and according to Wikipedia, the region was also inhabited by cocaine growers, paramilitary forces, guerrilla groups, military, indigenous Guahibo people, and others living near the border.

Paolo Lugari tried to bring everyone into the community, striving for equality among all. Many versions of wind power systems and pumps were developed to draw water from the ground.

At the time, some rainforests were being destroyed to make room for new housing. Lugari wanted to avoid this and instead use less environmentally sensitive areas, such as the Llanos, to establish a sustainable community.

The UNDP (United Nations Development Programme) was an early funder for the development of Gaviotas and praised the community for its windmill and water pump technology.

By the late 1970s, about 200 people had moved to live in Gaviotas.

A hospital was built, and an area with hammocks was added for Indigenous people to stay near their relatives, since the older part of the hospital felt too confining for many of them.

According to sources, some of the armed groups in the region fought each other, and the wounded from both sides were treated at the Gaviotas hospital—even while their enemies were being cared for nearby.

Gaviotas banned weapons within its area and remained neutral in politics, refusing to support one group over another. Several sources noted that most armed groups respected this stance, left the people of Gaviotas alone, and treated them peacefully.

Gaviotas: Innovation and Change

In the 1990s, the Colombian government forced the closing of the hospital. According to one source, the facility was then used to produce more biofuel, while another source states it was repurposed to purify water that was later bottled.

Early on, pine resin was sold for profit. However, when China flooded the market with cheaper pine resin, sales declined. The same source explains that later, purified water was bottled and sold to restaurants and retailers in other parts of Colombia. As part of a recycling program, these retailers and restaurants returned the bottles to Gaviotas as a condition of the sales agreement.

Some of the notable inventions included: a one-man manual cement mixer, a bicycle-like cassava grinder that could complete in one hour what previously took ten, a one-handed sugarcane press, and ponds constructed out of chicken wire and cement mixed with soil.

Paolo Lugari chose not to patent any of these technologies so that others could freely adopt and benefit from them.

In 1967, Paolo Lugari helped form an environmental and spiritual community in what was then a barren area.

The area where Gaviotas developed was part of the treeless plains known as the Llanos. Some sources say Gaviotas truly began in 1971.

Early in its history, solar energy was used to make water drinkable, and windmills were installed to generate power.

Pine trees from Honduras were introduced, though it took several attempts before the plantings succeeded. These trees were later used to produce instruments and turpentine, creating a source of commerce for the community.

The Llanos is also known as a grassland, and around Gaviotas, trees were planted to restore the area.

The Llanos region spans eastern Colombia and central Venezuela and lies east of the mountains.

A seesaw, originally used by children for recreation, was adapted to function as a pump to bring up water, which was later purified using solar power.

The Japanese government has been one of the donors to Gaviotas in support of its environmental initiatives.

Gaviotas now relies 100% on renewable energy, according to one source. Another source noted that it took 57 different designs to develop windmills that worked most effectively.

It was previously mentioned that the FARC and Red Brigade left the people of Gaviotas alone. One example given was when a leader of an armed group arrived with others carrying guns and asked, "Who is the leader of Gaviotas?" The response was, "We are all equal here; there is no leader. We make decisions by consensus."

Someone from Gaviotas then asked the group's leader if he intended to harm anyone or take anything. He replied that those in charge had instructed them to leave Gaviotas alone because the work being done there was valuable.

This is another account showing how Gaviotas was allowed to continue as a community, focusing on environmentally friendly technology and sustainable living.

Colombia's Political Turmoil and the Rise of Guerrilla Groups

According to Alan Weisman, who wrote *Gaviotas: A Village to Reinvent the World*:

From 1958 to 1974, the two main political parties (existing then) agreed to take turns every four years, alternating leadership.

After many years under a military dictatorship, during part of this era the indigenous people lost land to the wealthy aristocracy (often through insider deals).

Anti-government groups, such as guerrillas, also began to emerge.

FARC Or Revolutionary Armed Forces of Colombia – People's Army

They kidnapped a Peace Corps volunteer (from the U.S.) and held him in a tent for three years. Afterwards, the Peace Corps withdrew from Colombia. Another group, ELN (National Liberation Army), was thought to be inspired by Fidel Castro and Che Guevara. Another group, ELP (Maoist), was known as the People's Army of Liberation.

As mentioned before (written here by me earlier, and from a few sources), all these groups—whether guerrilla or army/police—

tended to leave Gaviotas alone. Gaviotas, the intentional community that carried out environmental science experiments, transformed a barren grassland (llanos) into a more forested and water-bearing area, bringing back plants that the indigenous people used for their folk (or real) medicine.

The Quakers have traditionally used consensus, where people negotiate and compromise. In my early experience with the Green Party in Virginia, we primarily used consensus, but as time went on we voted more often to get things done. If you can make decisions by consensus, you get the majority to buy into decisions, since they were directly involved in negotiation and compromise.

Greening the Llanos: Paolo Lugari's Vision

Paolo Lugari, who was the main leader of Gaviotas, had the idea to plant Caribbean pine trees in the barren llanos, which then only had grasses and small shrubs. The trees flourished, and the pine resin was turned into turpentine and sold to industry. As the trees thrived, native plants more accustomed to forests began sprouting up in the former grassland. Indigenous people rediscovered medicinal plants that had not been seen for years or were normally found only in jungle environments miles away. They were overjoyed to find these plants again.

The people of Gaviotas also planted palm trees, which were harvested to help make biodiesel to power machines. With this diversity of plants in the once-barren grassland, rainfall increased, water became more abundant, and some was filtered for people to drink (and bottled).

Sources:

https://mastersofbeautifulachievements.com/las-gaviotas-the-reforestation-miracle/

https://www.devalt.org/newsletter/jun09/of_2.htm

Gunter Pauli (http://www.zeri.org/forest.html), *scientist who studied and supported the llanos-to-forest transformation*

Gaviotas by Alan Weisman

Part of the resin from the pine trees planted in the former grassland was also made into fuel to power tractors and motorbikes.

https://www.100-percent.org/las-gaviotas-colombia/

https://theecologist.org/2010/jun/22/las-gaviotas-proving-sustainable-living-possible-where-it-shouldnt-be

Gaviotas: Innovation and Resilience in Colombia

Gaviotas, an intentional community, was founded in 1971 by Colombian politician Paolo Lugari. (It was discussed in the early 1980s during Green Party meetings.) The community had both environmental and spiritual leanings. One of its inventions was a seesaw that also functioned as a water pump—children could play on it while pumping water for use.

At the time, Colombia faced drug (cocaine) issues, and groups such as FARC (Revolutionary Armed Forces of Colombia), other non-government entities, and the Colombian army tended to leave the people of Gaviotas alone.

https://adamsulkowski.com/2019/05/13/50-years-of-green-entrepreneurship-with-paolo-lugari-founder-of-las-gaviotas-in-colombia-whom-gabriel-garcia-marquez-called-inventor-of-the-world/

From the pine trees, the community also developed a form of biodiesel called "energized pine oil." The government limited how much they could produce, though Gaviotas maintained it was less polluting than regular biodiesel.

https://rmi.org/blog_2013_11_12_a_high_renewables_tomorrow_today_gaviotas/

In a 2013 article, Laurie Stone noted that biodiesel produced in Gaviotas powers tractors, work trucks, and electric generators.

https://money.cnn.com/2007/09/26/technology/village_saving_planet.biz2/

Quote:

"Its products include a hydroelectric microturbine that generates 30 kilowatts and thousands of RPMs from a mere 1-meter drop in a low-fall dam."

Electricity Generation from Water

The article explains how a wind turbine is used to power a water pump that draws water from an aquifer. This water is bottled in a building in Gaviotas and sold in shops in Bogotá. It is also provided free of charge to the citizens of Gaviotas for drinking.

https://backspace.com/notes/2003/08/gaviotas.php

This article states that during the dry season, the hydroelectric microturbine does not receive enough water flow, so a biodiesel generator is used to provide electricity.

While the hospital existed (before being converted into a water bottling plant), underground ducts used wind from nearby hills to help cool the building.

https://www.latimes.com/archives/la-xpm-1994-09-25-tm-42932-story.html

The LA Times reported that Gaviotas had between 200 and 500 residents throughout the years.

Using reflective film and solar panels, Paolo Lugari and others from Gaviotas developed a solar technology that sterilized medical instruments at a hospital in Bogotá, the *Clínica San Pedro Claver*.

Gaviotas also used early solar technology for electricity and hot water, including in the hospital they built.

Gaviotas was partially funded by the United Nations Development Programme (UNDP). It again made use of windmills to power water pumps.

Recognition for Innovation

Gaviotas was awarded the 1997 World Prize in Zero Emissions by the United Nations' Zero Emissions Research Initiative.

From its beginning, Gaviotas employed innovative environmental techniques.

Gaviotas has been described as a self-sufficient reforestation community. Las Gaviotas is considered a model of a restorative enterprise.

Article by Adam Sulkowski, May 25, 2018.

Paolo Lugari estimated that Gaviotas was sequestering—by their calculations—89 tons of CO_2 for every 1 ton of CO_2 emitted.

The same article also quotes Gunter Pauli, speaking about Las Gaviotas:

"If it exists, then it must be possible."

Las Gaviotas and its people have deliberately never patented their know-how — all of it can be freely copied.

From *Permitting Nature to Pursue its Evolutionary Path by Prof. Gunter Pauli*:

Pauli stated that between 1984 and 2009, the number of plant species in Gaviotas increased from 17 (11 of them non-native) to 256.

In the 1980s, a hospital was built in Gaviotas that used innovative low-tech solutions for ventilation, such as sliding windows that allowed sunlight to kill germs.

The Colombian government—whether out of wisdom or interference—closed the hospital due to regulatory concerns.

The hospital building was later repurposed to bottle clean water, which is distributed free of charge to Gaviotas residents.

These three statements are from the article "Las Gaviotas: Sustainability in the Tropics" by Richard E. White and Gloria Eugenia Gonzales Marino.

Caribbean Pines and the Revival of the Llanos

Paolo Lugari planted 8,000 hectares of Caribbean pine trees in an area known as the *llanos*, which had been barren for about 100 years.

Mushroom mycelium (mycorrhizal fungi) was used to help the pine trees grow.

As stated before, the successful growth of these trees is believed to have increased rainfall by an estimated 10%, which contributed to the creation of drinking water sources and supported the growth of vegetation in what was once a barren landscape.

An estimated 260 different new plant species grew in this now fertile area—possibly due to birds dispersing seeds.

As previously mentioned, people who had lived in the area before the planting of pine trees recognized plants that they were familiar with—plants that had not grown in the barren llanos for many years. Some attributed the desert-like conditions to slash-and-burn farming techniques, which may have accelerated land degradation. These reappearing plants, found miles away in other regions, had both nutritional and medicinal value.

Wells of Innovation: Wind, Water, and Quiet Influence

Source:

- https://www.devalt.org/newsletter/jun09/of_2.htm
- https://en.wikipedia.org/wiki/Gaviotas#:~:text=Gaviotas%20has%20developed%20many%20internationally

Gaviotas also worked on various types of wind power systems and pumps to extract water from underground.

According to Wikipedia, various groups lived near or were associated with Gaviotas, including eco-anarchists, guerrilla groups (as mentioned previously), many of them armed, as well as members of the Colombian military.

As noted before, these groups generally left the intentional community of Gaviotas alone.

It is also reported that cattle farmers in nearby areas adopted water pump designs pioneered at Gaviotas. These pumps allowed them to access deeper underground aquifers during dry periods. The improved technology was more affordable than conventional pumps and was credited with reducing cattle mortality during droughts.

Sven Zethelius, who was Swedish-born, contributed to the development of soil cement, windmills, and water pumps for

Gaviotas. He also pioneered the technique of planting Caribbean pine tree seedlings together with mushroom mycelium, which significantly improved tree growth.

Inventing a Better World, One Mistake at a Time

According to Wikipedia, Paolo Lugari's uncle, Tomás Castrillón, suggested looking at land in the *llanos* region as a possible site for what would become Gaviotas.

Windmill development at Gaviotas involved testing 57 different prototypes to determine which design worked best.

Water pumps were also developed, including a sleeve pump capable of drawing water from greater depths. One innovative design repurposed a children's see-saw toy into a water pump—two children playing on the see-saw could power the mechanism to pump water.

Gaviotas also secured funding from investors to build a solar water heater factory in Bogotá. Small units were produced for individual use, while larger units were installed on a 5,500-room apartment complex in the city, with a large solar water heater placed on the roof.

Source:

https://theecologist.org/2010/jun/22/las-gaviotas-proving-sustainable-living-possible-where-it-shouldnt-be

(This article provides details on the factory and apartment complex that used technology developed at Gaviotas.)

Gabriel García Márquez, the famous author of *One Hundred Years of Solitude,* called Paolo Lugari the "Inventor of the World."

Gunter Pauli, a Belgian-born scientist who visited Gaviotas in 1984, praised the people who worked on technology there for never copyrighting their inventions. One of his quotes:

"All of it can be freely copied."

One website states that Gunter Pauli has visited Gaviotas over 12 times.

Source:
https://www.devalt.org/newsletter/jun09/of_2.htm

That same website also explains that by planting trees in the dry, barren *llanos*, Gaviotas helped regenerate the land. As vegetation returned, new sources of water emerged to serve the surrounding community.

The site further states that the intentional community of Gaviotas provides:

"Every family has free housing, community meals, and schooling. There are no weapons, no police, no jail or rules, yet they are an oasis of peace."

It also includes quotes from Paolo Lugari:

"The fastest way to become successful is to make lots of mistakes."

"Gaviotas is not a community that can be replicated. What needs to be replicated is the Gaviotas way of thinking."

"Civilization has been a permanent dialogue between human beings and water."

"There's no such thing as sustainable technology or economic development without sustainable human development to match."

Sources:

https://laotzu.xyz/author/display?id=424

http://www.indiaenvironmentportal.org.in/files/World%20Watch1.pdf

World Watch Magazine
By Richard E. White and Gloria Eugenia González Marino
May–June 2007

This article praises a solar water heater system whose technology was used in Bogotá (previously mentioned in earlier manuscripts). It was notable for having no moving parts.

"A solar hot water system for Ciudad Tunal, a 6,000-apartment public housing project in Bogotá."

The article later states that the solar water heater still works perfectly—despite being installed years earlier.

It also discusses a hospital built in the 1980s and closed in the 1990s by decree of the Colombian government. After its closure, the building was repurposed for bottling safe drinking water, which is distributed free to local residents.

According to the article, the rural hospital was closed because it was deemed not economically viable by the government. Notably, the hospital used subsurface tunnels for ventilation—a low-tech but effective innovation.

A Conversation with Paolo Lugari, Founder of Las Gaviotas, Colombia

The *llanos* (a formerly desert-like area where Lugari planted pine trees with mushroom mycelium wrapped around the roots to aid growth) are located in eastern Colombia and western Venezuela.

Source:
https://www.zermattsummit.org/news/the-man-who-brought-back-a-rainforest/

According to the article, Lugari was 72 years old in 2020.

Originally, there were only 20 plant species in the llanos; 50 years later, that number had increased to 250.

Lugari states that trees not only absorb CO_2 from the atmosphere but also help restore the soil.

As mentioned earlier, the trees and newly emerged plant species also helped improve the water table. The article notes that bottled water from Gaviotas is now sold in restaurants in Bogotá.

Additionally, Lugari distributes notebooks made from "stone paper"—a type of paper produced using calcium carbonate instead of traditional wood pulp.

Source:
https://en.wikipedia.org/wiki/Gaviotas

Gaviotas—and Paolo Lugari—proposed a theory that technology for emerging or poor nations must be inexpensive and, ideally, labor-intensive, so that more people can be involved in the work.

No patents were ever applied for the many low-tech inventions developed at Gaviotas.

A total of 57 windmill prototypes were tested before version number 58, which worked best—demonstrating their willingness to keep experimenting and evolving.

I've always been amazed by the see-saw water pump—a children's play toy made useful for drawing water.

(Jim Lowenstern)

Source: *Las Gaviotas: Proving Sustainable Living Possible Where It Shouldn't Be*

Forty years ago, a brilliant young dreamer, Paolo Lugari, decided that he wanted to turn the dream of sustainability into reality. While flying over the "wet desert" of Los Llanos in his native Colombia, he was struck by a vision: if it was possible to live sustainably there, it could be done anywhere.

Gathering a team of scientists, artists, and indigenous Guahibo people, they founded a community—Gaviotas—that has consistently achieved the impossible, innovating and adapting decade after decade.

—*Quote from source:*

https://img1.wsimg.com/blobby/go/f95d9579-7769-48b8-aeec-8c1b10bddd91/downloads/achievements.pdf?ver=1740808181584

HEALTH

Development and application of appropriate technologies for primary healthcare

These consist of small, low-cost modules—simple, easy to maintain, and accessible to the social and environmental conditions of the humid tropics. Many of the instructions were translated into the local indigenous language, Sikuani.

A self-sufficient 16-bed hospital was also built and operated for 20 years. It provided primary-level care and applied appropriate technologies. However, the Colombian government eventually forced its closure, and the building was repurposed as a water treatment facility.

RENEWABLE ENERGIES

Gaviotas developed numerous innovative technologies, including:

1. Tropical solar water heaters (100% solar-powered, with no moving parts). Over 35,000 units have been manufactured and installed. In Ciudad Tunal, south of Bogotá, 5,000 units were installed—making it the largest concentration of solar water heaters in a single neighborhood globally.

2. Compact solar boiler for a single-family household, producing 8 gallons of drinkable water daily, powered entirely by solar energy. It has only one moving part—a float.

3. Environmental solar heaters designed and produced for homes and offices.

4. Solar stove using thermo-oil, fueled by cottonseed oil. Heated by high-performance solar collectors, the stove operates both day and night due to an insulated tank. It features four double-bottomed containers.

5. Interactive solar energy module designed and built for a museum in Bogotá.

6. Tropical windmill with a double-effect mechanism for extracting water—designed without the need for a steering vane. Approximately 5,000 units have been manufactured and installed, mostly in remote rural areas of Colombia.

7. Manual "shirt pumps" (a type of hand pump for deep wells up to 40 meters). In these pumps, the external pipe ("shirt") moves instead of the piston. When combined, two shirt pumps were used to create a school see-saw that also pumps water—a widely adopted innovation in rural schools. In total, about 15,000 pumps and see-saws have been manufactured and installed.

8. Improved hydraulic ram pumps, powered solely by the force of falling water, requiring no fossil fuels. Over 9,000 units have been installed.

9. Remote-control manual pump, allowing residents to pump water from their homes without going to the well. It uses a hydraulic control system connected through above- and below-ground pipes.

10. Axial hydraulic microturbines (2 to 30 kW capacity), designed to provide electricity to isolated homes in tropical regions using small waterfalls.

11. Biomass power plant (150 kW capacity), fueled by biomass sourced from the pruning of Gaviotas' tropical plantations, used to generate steam for electricity.

These inventions and innovations are detailed in the source:

https://img1.wsimg.com/blobby/go/f95d9579-7769-48b8-aeec-8c1b10bddd91/downloads/achievements.pdf?ver=1740808181584

Also referenced by the Gaviotas Community - Global Earth Repair Foundation.

--

The pines are slowly being crowded out by the regeneration of indigenous species. The community is generating power using turbine engines fueled by the aging pines in their forest. Since already-existing solutions are often very costly to adapt, Gaviotas' innovations are usually simple modifications to production methods that make otherwise expensive products available at affordable prices.

—Quote from source:

"The only fixed idea in Gaviotas," states Lugari, "is that nothing is done that is not sustainable in the final balance."

—Quote from:

https://rmi.org/blog_2013_11_12_a_high_renewables_tomorrow_today_gaviotas/

FRED CUNY

The Death of Fred Cuny

Sometime in April 1995, according to witnesses, a 50-year-old Texan named Fred Cuny was ordered to his knees and shot in the head in a remote corner of Chechnya. To this day, no one knows for certain why Chechen gunmen killed Cuny—only that the death of this man, who spent 25 years alleviating the world's worst disasters, remains an incalculable loss.

Fred Cuny worked on humanitarian aid projects in countries affected by disasters. He was born on November 14, 1944, and is believed to have died on March 31, 1995—possibly at the hands of Chechen fighters or the Russian military, which was engaged in a brutal conflict with Chechnya at the time. The exact circumstances of his death remain unknown.

Early Humanitarian Work

Cuny traveled to various parts of the world to help people suffering from famine, war, and natural disasters. Some of the places he worked include:

- Biafra (during the Nigerian Civil War in the late 1960s)
- Guatemala (following the 1976 earthquake)
- Kuwait (in 1991, after the Gulf War)
- Iran (in 1992, following an earthquake)

Fred Cuny wrote a book: *Famine, Conflict, and Response: A Basic Guide*

Website Sections:

Home · Who Killed Fred Cuny · Map of Cuny's World · From His Laptop · On the Life · His Radio Interviews · Special Reports · Friends & Colleagues · Links · Viewer Discussion · Press Reaction · Tapes & Transcripts

Early Life and Education

A great TV documentary was made about Fred Cuny.

Fred Cuny was at Texas A&M University. He wanted to become a Marine pilot, but one source said he was too tall to qualify. He left college after a fire broke out in his dormitory. Some claimed he caused it, while others said he knew who started the fire but refused to tell.

It's stated that he did serve as a Marine. However, after he broke a leg in an accident involving a reportedly drunk taxi driver, he was medically discharged from the U.S. Marine Corps. It's said that for about a month afterward, Cuny experienced a personal crisis.

In 1969, Fred Cuny went to Biafra, a breakaway territory from Nigeria. He helped coordinate airlift operations in jungle areas to deliver food to starving people. This early experience planted the seed for Cuny's later concepts on how to assist displaced populations and organize refugee camps.

Formation of Intertect

After returning to Texas, Cuny founded a company called *Intertect*, which specialized in disaster response. Initially, the company made no profit, and Cuny supported himself by flying small planes in the summer to spray crops for farmers.

Intertect helped organize three major conferences focused on building safer housing in earthquake-prone regions. One of the techniques promoted was using locally sourced mud materials to build more stable homes. During this time, he visited many nations, working with local builders to teach his construction theories and promote safer, culturally adapted building practices.

Major Disaster Relief Missions

In 1976, a major earthquake struck Guatemala. Cuny flew his Cessna from Dallas to Guatemala, where nearly a million people were left homeless. He tried to implement temporary housing using corrugated metal, with mixed success. He often clashed with other NGO groups, who did not see eye to eye with his methods. Cuny remained an independent contractor throughout.

In 1985, during the Ethiopian famine, many people fled to Sudan. Cuny went there and proposed organizing refugee camps in circular patterns instead of grids. He believed that politics, tribalism, and international rivalries were contributing to the crisis. He again clashed with others in the humanitarian field but helped develop a 50-day food package that included seeds and tools for people willing to return to Ethiopia.

Near the end of Saddam Hussein's rule in Iraq, the Kurds had fled to the mountains of Turkey. Cuny did something controversial: he encouraged U.S. Marines to escort the Kurds back to their homes in northern Iraq, as Hussein was being defeated by U.S. forces. It was said that Cuny "borrowed" some Marines and successfully facilitated the return of some Kurdish families. Some in the military were reportedly unhappy with his ingenuity and initiative.

Battle of Mogadishu

The Battle of Mogadishu, also known as "Black Hawk Down," occurred during a U.S.-led UN intervention in Somalia, part of Operation Restore Hope, which aimed to protect humanitarian aid efforts.

During the Battle of Mogadishu on October 3–4, 1993, 18 U.S. soldiers were killed, along with hundreds of Somali militia fighters and civilians, in a major engagement during the Somali Civil War.

Fred Cuny wrote a strategic plan for this situation nearly a year earlier, on November 21, 1992.

It was five pages long and contained 11 key points.

One person commented that Cuny had advised the U.S. military not to send forces into Mogadishu. Tragically, this advice was ignored.

Another person, quoting from globalideasbank.org/inspir/INS-179. HTML, wrote:

"In spite of wide circulation of the Cuny plan amongst U.S. politicians and favorable editorials in several American newspapers, nearly every point in Cuny's list of suggestions was flatly ignored by military planners..."

Cuny first observed the Biafra situation in 1969. He attempted to assist both sides of the conflict, but the Nigerian government rejected his help. He then focused on aiding the Biafrans—i.e., the Republic of Biafra, which was trying to secede from Nigeria. Many of those attempting to establish Biafra were from the Ibo (Igbo) ethnic group.

It is said that Cuny was dissatisfied with the drainage and sanitation conditions in refugee camps, particularly the latrines, which were causing flooding and poor hygiene. In response, he brought in engineers to help improve these conditions. This experience helped inspire him to form his company, *Intertect*, which focused on refugee camp design and disaster response.

Cuny developed a theory, one that frustrated him off and on, that food is often hoarded during famines. He believed that, if funding could be secured, it might be possible to redistribute that food. This theory appeared to hold true in some tent city and refugee camp situations, but not in others.

***

Heat and Hope for Sarajevo

The Serbians blockaded food shipments intended for the Bosnians— aid that had been provided by other nations.

Intertect, the company Fred Cuny founded to provide humanitarian aid worldwide, was working with the IRC (International Rescue Committee) during the Sarajevo crisis.

Using part of George Soros's $50 million donation designated for aid to the Bosnians, Cuny brought 15 miles of reinforced plastic piping into the area.

Cuny and his team at Intertect also developed a gas stove that doubled as a heater for use in the besieged city.

A quote from Aryeh Neier, who helped manage Soros's humanitarian funding:

"Fred managed to enlist 15,000 Sarajevans to dig trenches through the streets to put in the gas lines—and this was while the shelling was taking place."

Quote sourced from the book:

The Man Who Tried to Save the World: The Dangerous Life & Mysterious Disappearance of Fred Cuny

by Scott Anderson

Restoring Sarajevo: Cuny's Lifeline

Cuny decided that, instead of spreading Soros's money thinly throughout Bosnia, it should be concentrated on restoring basic utilities in Sarajevo, including water, gas, and electricity. At the end of 1993, I flew to Sarajevo with Soros, Neier, and Rosenblatt. The huge Russian transport plane, hired by the UN, was filled with iron piping, purchased by Soros, which was to be used for one of Fred Cuny's plans: restoring the gas pipelines running through the city so that people could heat their apartments. The freezing cold had been destroying lives, and morale was desperately low.

This illustrates how Cuny consistently thought outside the box, finding practical solutions to critical problems.

Water was pumped up from the river below the road. In the tunnel, it first passed through a "skid" consisting of three chemical containers, which added a flocculant, a substance that gathered the dirt and other suspended particles into small clumps. The liquid was then sprayed onto a clarifier, where the heavier material was separated into a sludge line; this sludge was pumped into the storm-sewer system and returned to the river.

The clarified water then passed through three filters: anthracite, sand, and garnet; it was subsequently chlorinated and pumped up the hill to an old reservoir, built during the Austro-Hungarian Empire. This reservoir had been abandoned for years until Cuny had it restored. From there, the water flowed by gravity through the city. The project, an impressive combination of ancient and modern engineering, cost only $2.5 million.

Again, this effort highlights Cuny's technical ingenuity. Despite many struggles, he succeeded in getting safe, clean water through the pipes to the people living in Sarajevo.

In 1993, Fred Cuny had filters flown in from Texas to supply clean water to the people of Sarajevo. It appears that both the Serbs and the Bosnians were accused of shutting off the water filtration system that Cuny had temporarily repaired.

Engineering Relief in Sarajevo

George Soros funded Cuny's efforts to repair both water and gas lines in Sarajevo. Cuny used this funding to pay local residents to dig trenches, and he installed plastic and iron piping. As a result, the percentage of people in and around Sarajevo with access to gas for heating and cooking increased from 10% to 60%.

Cuny also designed a small gas-powered heater that doubled as a stove. He arranged for a nearby factory to produce the units, giving people in the war-torn area access to heat and a better means to cook food.

In addition, Cuny devised a 200-meter water filtration system using a tunnel next to the river, allowing people to have clean water—at least for a time.

More information on the water filtration system and expanded access to gas lines organized by Cuny can be found here:

https://www.opensocietyfoundations.org/voices/helping-balkans-survive-decade-war

***

Each year, thousands of experienced relief workers are actively prevented from helping the displaced by the very governments they seek to assist. If the displaced choose to remain in rebel-held areas...

-Fred Cuny

He went on to criticize the United Nations, suggesting it was ineffective in addressing these challenges.

Cuny also pointed out that indigenous people living in jungles and rural areas in countries like Africa, Brazil, and Indonesia were being threatened by their own governments. He stated that indigenous groups:

"...face extinction because of persecution by their governments."

Cuny had strong theories and ideas on how to improve humanitarian response efforts but lacked the power to implement them fully, which was a frequent frustration in his work.

Fred Cuny wrote a book titled Famine, Conflict and Response: A Basic Guide

(Page 13, Cuny cites: P. Cutler,

The Use of Economic and Social Information in Famine Prediction and Response

September 1985)

Cutler Chart

The first item on the chart is the cause and nature of famine, including war, etc.

The second item, which Cuny often quotes, is a three-part concept; the first element in the chart is hoarding by various entities.

Cuny frequently suggested funding such businesses to help release goods and food to starving people, as an example.

The second item on the chart is inflation.

The third item is loss of job or livelihood.

The Cutler chart then expands into three more areas related to the points made above.

Cuny attempted to address issues such as gas in plumbing, water drainage, and availability of clean, safe drinking water. He also worked on latrine issues, developed a solar oven, and designed a combined heater/stove powered by gas—which he installed in many homes by providing the pipes and manpower.

More information can be found here:

https://fredcuny.info/influence/

This manual for architects begins by examining the work of three engineers—William LeMessurier, Roger Boisjoly, and Frederick C. Cuny—whose contributions are widely regarded as ethically exemplary. The book aims to present the best tools for achieving the highest ethical standards and practices, while also helping readers understand the critical role that future professional engineers play in safeguarding the health, safety, and welfare of the public and the environment.

Engineering Ethics: Concepts and Cases, by Charles E. Harris Jr., Michael S. Pritchard, Michael J. Rabins, Washington State University, Biological Systems Engineering, 2009

The authors attribute credit to Fred Cuny for many of the principles cited in this book.

Transitional Settlement: Displaced Populations, by Tom Corsellis and Antonella Vitale, Oxfam, 2005

Fred Cuny significantly influenced Maynard's work as a mentor, colleague, and member of her doctoral committee.

Healing Communities in Conflict: International Assistance in Complex Emergencies, by Kimberly A. Maynard, Columbia University Press, New Edition, 2002

It was essentially Fred Cuny's idea, and it led directly to the development of the SPHERE standards (acknowledged in the first edition but not in subsequent editions).

The first three are structured around case studies: convoys to Goražde (land), airdrops (air), and Fred Cuny's water project in Sarajevo (water).

https://www.urban-response.org/system/files/content/resource/files/main/pdacj890.pdf

Foundations of Ethical Engineering

On the ground, relief expert Fred Cuny realized what had happened and coined the phrase "humanitarian air cover." This occurs when the protection of military assets engaged in a humanitarian mission requires a more aggressive military deployment—typically from the air—which, in turn, intimidates forces on the ground that are guilty of abusing civilian populations. Other new concepts were gaining ground, such as the idea of "preventive protection"—the protection offered by the mere presence of international personnel.

22 Cuny, F.C. (with F. Brilliant, P. Reed, and V. Tanner): Humanitarian Intervention: A Study of Operation Provide Comfort, unpublished report, INTERTECT (Dallas, TX), 1995: pp. 70–71.

Cuny coined the phrase "humanitarian air cover." He thought it so important that he justified the mountain airdrops, which had been, from a relief operations point of view, disastrous. Cuny sought, unsuccessfully, to convince U.S. policymakers to apply the concept in Bosnia.

Source: <u>Urban Response</u> – <u>https://www.urban-response.org/system/files/content/resource/files/main/pdacj890.pdf</u>

By late 1994, several other NGOs had the size and operational infrastructure to implement major programs in Bosnia. CRS, Mercy Corps, and LMCOR were among those funded by OFDA. Other OFDA grantees, such as AICF and Solidarités, attempted to avoid the "growth trap" and maintained targeted, effective, albeit less ambitious, programs. The IRC continued with its important agricultural (seed) and local production initiatives.

In Sarajevo, spurred the INTERTECT—the small Dallas-based consulting firm led by innovative relief expert Fred Cuny—and with funding from the Soros Foundation, IRC advanced groundbreaking municipal gas and water programs, which were designed and managed by Cuny. Nevertheless, the field had broadened.

43 International financier George Soros donated $50 million to UNHCR for NGO programs, in an effort to pressure the agency to streamline its funding of NGOs. The trust fund was administered in part by UNHCR, with technical advice from the experienced and well-respected relief expert Fred Cuny.

Source: <u>Urban Response</u> – <u>https://www.urban-response.org/system/files/content/resource/files/main/pdacj890.pdf</u>

Key References:

Cuny, F.C.: An Assessment of Airdrops in Relief Operations, unpublished manuscript, INTERTECT (Dallas, TX), 23 August 1994.

Cuny, F.C. (with F. Brilliant, P. Reed, and V. Tanner): Humanitarian Intervention: A Study of Operation Provide Comfort, INTERTECT (Dallas, TX), 1995.

Cuny, F.C.: "Working with Local Communities to Reduce Conflict: Spot Reconstruction," Disaster Prevention and Management Journal, Vol. 4, UK, 1995.

More Information on Cuny's Knowledge and Contributions

As stated before, Cuny favored circular designs over traditional straight lines for tents.

It was said to improve social structure.

In 1985, in Sudan, he worked with Ethiopian refugees.

In Nicaragua (1972) and Thailand (1979), he got impoverished communities and/or refugees involved—with help—in building the housing they needed to shelter themselves. Cuny designed a more efficient refugee camp layout. He improved latrines and installed functional water systems, ensuring people had access to safe drinking water.

At least twice, Cuny led refugee populations back to the areas of their former homes. In one case—Sudan to Ethiopia in 1985—he helped people return to areas controlled by hostile forces that didn't want them there. He provided seeds so they could grow food in gardens and farmland.

In parts of Iraq, according to several sources, he used the U.S. military to help bring the Kurds back to where they used to live, instead of leaving them in refugee camps.

In Sarajevo, for example, Cuny chose to improve existing housing rather than starting from scratch. As mentioned previously, he installed new or upgraded gas lines and designed small gas-powered heaters and stoves to improve quality of life.

(some link or picture is inserted here "Fred Cuny's life event)

The text above states that Fred Cuny met George Soros, who funded Cuny's work or attempts to help in the Sarajevo situation from 1993 to 1996.

Cuny had his company, Intertect.

It also states that Soros asked Cuny to go help in Chechnya (where Cuny eventually died).

It is believed that Cuny died in late March or early April 1995 during the Russian–Chechen conflict.

https://www.nybooks.com/articles/1999/12/02/life-and-death-of-a-hero/

The above article states that Aryeh Neier, who headed a project for George Soros, said he asked Cuny to help in Sarajevo.

https://www.pbs.org/wgbh/pages/frontline/shows/cuny/laptop/waterproject.html

(As mentioned before, Cuny used a tunnel near Sarajevo to build a water treatment plant.)

***

The Moment of Truth

(insert some link / picture here from ms)

Washington Post, 1995

A quote from George Soros in the article:

"The only supply of water and electricity currently available in Sarajevo was installed by Fred Cuny, our disaster expert who is now missing in Chechnya."

TV, Frontline on Cuny

https://onlineethics.org/cases/engineers-and-scientists-behaving-well/fred-cuny-1944-1995-disaster-relief-innovator

Timeline Overview of Fred Cuny's Humanitarian Work

Biafra/Nigeria, 1969

Cuny was at an airport near Biafra and Nigeria during the Biafran conflict. He was helping the Biafrans by delivering aid. A plane delivering this aid crashed while landing at the airport, effectively closing it down.

The mercenaries who opposed helping Biafra realized that the closed airport was affecting their own paychecks. In response, they bombed the already-damaged aid plane on the runway—ironically allowing the airport to reopen and resume operations. This incident illustrates the strange and often cynical dynamics of the aid and conflict situation in the region.

Cuny was not satisfied with the drainage and sanitation conditions. He worked directly with people on the ground to improve these issues.

He also arranged for food to be delivered to rural locations instead of forcing everyone to go to the airport for distribution.

Guatemala Earthquake, 1976

Results were mixed. Cuny was unhappy with the aid response focused on housing reconstruction. To help volunteers build or rebuild collapsed housing, he created a comic-style instruction manual and taught improved construction techniques.

Unfortunately, a faction of the government—or the existing government itself—feared the volunteer-led effort. This fear led to threats and even acts of violence against people trying to rebuild, possibly due to perceived threats to the political status quo.

Ethiopia/Sudan Famine, 1985

Cuny reorganized refugee camps from a rigid grid layout into a circular design, which he believed worked better socially and functionally for refugees.

He also went against the opinion of some aid workers in the camps by encouraging people to return to Ethiopia. While others feared for the safety of returning to a war-torn area, Cuny helped provide supplies and seeds for those willing to go. The rains eventually came, and many of the people who followed Cuny's advice were successful, growing food on their land.

Iraq, 1991

During the Saddam Hussein era, the Kurds fled Iraq and took refuge in Turkey. The Turkish government was unhappy about this at the time—and reportedly remains unhappy about it even today.

Cuny somehow got the U.S. military to help escort a large number of Kurds back to the areas in Iraq where they once lived. Some people were upset with Cuny for involving the U.S. military to ensure this worked out, while others remain amazed that he was able to make the desired outcome happen.

He later airlifted supplies to camps established along the route back home. This operation became known as "Operation Provide Comfort."

Somalia, 1992 – Famine and Civil War

Cuny was in Somalia during the crisis. His goal was to establish temporary housing away from Mogadishu, which he believed was too dangerous due to ongoing conflict. He submitted a proposal to the U.S. military outlining his recommendations, but it was ignored.

Instead, the U.S. attempted to enter Mogadishu directly, which led to tragic consequences. The situation, even today, remains far from ideal.

***

"The airfield was effectively closed. There was no way we could get in and out. There wasn't enough room. Everybody said, 'This is going to take a long time... maybe tractors could pull it off.'

We were sitting there the next morning doing an assessment: 'What are we going to do about this, and how do we get this thing off?' And we looked up, and here come two MiG-17s. They flew over, sort of came in close for a look, and then they went back.

Then about two hours later, they came back with bombs and just proceeded to bomb the hell out of the airplane—broke it into nice little pieces so we could clear it off the runway and get back in operation."

-Fred Cuny

***

They clearly knew that if it was over, that their bread ticket was going to be punched and that would be it. So, in many ways, the Nigerians certainly were not well served by the people they hired. They could have stopped us.

-Fred Cuny

Challenging Aid Norms

Nigeria did not want Biafra to secede, and as mentioned above, mercenaries played a role in keeping the airport open—not out of humanitarian concern, but to ensure they still had jobs and pay.

In the same account, Cuny shared an early insight that would shape much of his later work:

He noted that "there is always food where people are starving"—highlighting that famine is often not about lack of food, but about economic access and logistics. He was deeply dissatisfied with the system that required refugees to come to airports for food distribution. Instead, Cuny wanted to deliver food directly to those in need in the countryside.

He was also unhappy with the flooding and high rates of diarrhea in tent cities and refugee camps—conditions he encountered repeatedly in disaster zones. These themes would come up again in his later work, as he consistently tried to solve or alleviate such problems during his disaster relief efforts.

Other Contributions

Cuny often worked directly with local builders and citizens, using local materials adapted to make structures more resilient. He prioritized building techniques that improved structural safety, especially in disaster-prone areas.

In Guatemala and Haiti, Cuny used multi-language instructional materials—combining local and indigenous languages—in a format that resembled comic books. This approach made it easier for communities to understand basic building concepts and empowered them to construct safer homes themselves.

He also worked on improving masonry techniques, such as producing better bricks, and retrofitted existing houses to increase their chances of withstanding future earthquakes.

In 1980, he traveled to Somalia to assist refugees coming from Ethiopia.

Additional Locations:
Kuwait, 1991
Iran, 1992

CONCLUSION

Across continents and disciplines, through the lens of faith, sustainability, and humanitarian engineering, three men stood as unlikely companions in a shared mission: Padre Pio, Paolo Lugari, and Fred Cuny. Their lives did not intersect in time or place. Yet their actions echo the same fundamental truth: hope can be engineered, cultivated, or prayed into being. But it must be acted upon.

At first glance, their vocations could not be more different. Padre Pio, cloaked in the silence of a monastery in southern Italy, tended to the souls of the suffering. Paolo Lugari, confronting ecological and political desolation, imagined a thriving, sustainable village in Colombia's least promising landscape. Fred Cuny, armed with blueprints and bold ideas, brought clean water, warmth, and dignity to war zones and refugee camps the world had largely forgotten.

Yet beneath the differences lay striking parallels.

They each chose to work on the frontlines of hardship. Not where recognition waited, but where needs were greatest. They embraced unconventional thinking, refusing to accept that the way things were was the way they had to be. They each followed a moral compass not dictated by institutions or ideology, but rooted in conscience, justice, and service.

Their legacy is not only in what they built or healed, but in what they made possible: lives lived with dignity, even in the face of chaos. Padre Pio's presence continues to offer solace. Lugari's Gaviotas continues to grow. Cuny's methods continue to save lives. These are not static legacies. They are living testaments to the power of action rooted in compassion.

Where others saw failure or futility, these men saw possibility. And they dared to act.

Their stories leave us with a profound message: the tools of compassion may differ, but the mission remains the same. A priest, an inventor, and a disaster engineer remind us that no field is beyond the reach of humanity. In a world that often glorifies individualism and short-term gain, their lives quietly declare something far more radical:

To serve is to hope.

To create is to heal.

To act is to believe.

www.ingramcontent.com/pod-product-compliance
Lightning Source LLC
Chambersburg PA
CBHW061719120626
46550CB00003B/1294